A Heritage Project of The Toronto and Region Conservation Authority

Black Creek Pioneer Village

NICK MIKA
HELMA MIKA
GARY THOMPSON

NATURAL HERITAGE BOOKS
TORONTO

This edition © 2000 Natural Heritage Books
All rights reserved. No portion of this book, with the exception of brief extracts for the purpose of literary or scholarly review, may be reproduced in any form without the permission of the publisher.

Published by Natural Heritage/Natural History Inc.
P.O. Box 95, Station O, Toronto, Ontario M4A 2M8

Cover design by Blanche Hamill, Norton Hamill Design.
This edition edited by Jane Gibson.
Printed and bound in Canada by Hignell Printing Limited.

Canadian Cataloguing in Publication Data

Mika, Nick, 1912–
    Black Creek Pioneer Village : Toronto's living history village

Rev. ed.
Includes index.
ISBN 1-896219-64-0

1. Black Creek Pioneer Village (Toronto, Ont.). 2. North York (Toronto, Ont.)–Buildings, structures, etc. 3. Black Creek Pioneer Village (Toronto, Ont.)–Pictorial works. I. Mika, Helma, 1924– . II. Thomson, Gary, 1943– . III. Title.

FC3065.B63M55 2000   971.3'541   C00-931021-5
F1059.52.M55 2000

The Canada Council | Le Conseil des Arts
    for the Arts | du Canada
    since 1957 | depuis 1957

Natural Heritage/Natural History Inc. acknowledges the support received for its publishing program from the Canada Council Block Grant Program and the assistance of the Association for the Export of Canadian Books, Ottawa. Natural Heritage also acknowledges the support of the Ontario Council for the Arts for its publishing program.

Dedicated to Russell King Cooper
1926–1999

Russ Cooper, on Queen Street, waiting for a wagon ride. Welcome to Black Creek Pioneer Village. Explore and enjoy.

A journalist, a photographer, a genealogist, an historian, a collector, a gardener, a volunteer, a true Canadian and a gentleman, Russell King Cooper was the guiding force behind Black Creek Pioneer Village from 1965 to 1991.

Russell Cooper was a man with a vision, a vision that steered Black Creek Pioneer Village for over 25 years through its most dynamic period of growth and development. Ever grateful to those who preceded him for their foresight and diligence in creating the Village, Russell, as its Administrator, led the fledgling site to maturity.

Following a well-defined master plan, he added over 30 buildings and structures, seeking out appropriate additions, encouraging and developing support and special interest groups. As well, he oversaw the relocations, the restorations, the furnishings, the landscaping and the interpretation. During his administration almost 7,000,000 visitors came to the Village to enjoy the fruits of his labour. He had a passion for, and an extensive knowledge of, Ontario history and his name was synonymous with heritage preservation throughout the Province. His avid collecting and exceptional reputation encouraged the donations of many thousands of artifacts to the Village. The extensive collection today housed at the site is a tribute to his efforts on behalf of preserving Ontario's past for the future.

It is with gratitude and affection that this publication is dedicated to the memory of Russell King Cooper.

Contents

Foreword 11

Map of Black Creek Pioneer Village 13

The Village 15

The Stong Settlement and Life on the Farm 17

The Gristmill 28

Other Early Industries and Crafts 31

The Homes of Some Villagers 39

The Laskay Emporium and Post Office 45

The Herb Garden 47

The Half Way House 48

Dickson's Hill School 50

Religious Life 53

The Town Hall 55

A Woman's Work is Never Done 56

Black Creek Pioneer Village in Colour 57

Bibliography 104

Index 105

Foreword

"It is only by looking into the past that one sees the future"
Sir Winston Churchill

One cannot deal successfully with the present or the future without understanding the past. True understanding comes from experiencing—Black Creek presents experiences. From the first step onto the wooden boardwalk, time changes. The smell of cooking, the sound of the blacksmith hammering on his anvil, the feel of soft fleece, the taste of fresh whole wheat bread and the sight of crinolined skirts swaying along the pathways, all help to erase the modern world for a short while. The visitor no longer merely views but participates—history has become an experience involving all the senses.

In 1956 few people realized what was to develop from a little Pioneer Museum housed in the Dalziel Barn. Located way out in the country north of Toronto at the intersection of two unpaved roads, who could visualize to what extent both the museum and the city would flourish and grow. Fortunately men and women with foresight and dedication were involved with the museum from the beginning. In their collection of, and care for, early local agricultural artifacts they planted the seeds which were to grow into a complete picture of life in early rural Ontario. Every year thousands of visitors enjoy the thrill of "stepping back in time" at Black Creek Pioneer Village, Toronto's living history village, a heritage project of the Toronto and Region Conservation Authority.

Lorraine O'Byrne
Curator
Black Creek Pioneer Village

Map of Black Creek Pioneer Village

1. Daniel Stong's Grain Barn
2. The Fire House
3. The Harness Shop and Saddlery
4. The Apple Storage Cellar
5. The Chicken House
6. Daniel Stong's Piggery
7. Daniel Stong's First House
8. Daniel Stong's Smoke House
9. Henry Snider's Backhouse
10. Daniel Stong's Second House
11. Laskay Emporium and Post Office
12. Half Way House Bake Oven
13. Limehouse Backhouse
14. Half Way House
15. Rose Blacksmith Shop
16. The Daniel Flynn Home
17. Burwick Home
18. Dickson's Hill School
19. Roblin's Mill
20. Richmond Hill Manse
21. Church Drive Shed
22. Fisherville Church
23. Taylor Cooperage
24. Daniel Flynn Boot and Shoe Shop
25. Dominion Carriage Works
26. Cabinet Maker's Shop
27. The Doctor's Home
28. Black Creek Printing Office
29. Charles Irvine's Weavers Shop
30. Mackenzie Home
31. Mackenzie Barn
32. The Town Hall
33. The Town Hall Drive Shed
34. The Gunsmith's Shop
35. Edgely Mennonite Meeting House Drive Shed
36. Edgely Mennonite Meeting House
37. The Broom Maker's Shop
38. The Edgely Slaughter House
39. Drive Shed
40. Henry Snider's Cider Mill
41. The Tinsmith Shop and The Black Creek Masonic Lodge

Daniel Stong's Houses

The Village

In the northwest corner of the bustling city of Toronto stands Black Creek Pioneer Village, a replica of a typical 19th century crossroads settlement in southern Ontario. The village, laid out on a 56-acre site, welcomes thousands of visitors each year to its peaceful rural setting. As they pass through the toll gate, they are at once entering a different world.

Within the confines of the village the sounds and sights of another age are in sharp contrast to the towering buildings and the noise of 21st century traffic on nearby Jane Street and Steeles Avenue. At Black Creek the pace is slower, reminiscent of a time when travel was measured in days, not in hours, and when life was harder and simpler but rewarding.

As you walk down the dusty road along Queen Street you find yourself drawn into the life of this pleasant little community until you become a part of it and the gentle rhythms of its activities take you far back in time.

You pass the harness shop and saddlery. Outside an old dog is lying in the sun, waiting for his master who is inside to have the harness repaired for his team of horses. An apprentice hurries by on an errand for his employer.

Two ladies wearing sunbonnets and bright gingham dresses walk toward the Laskay Emporium. Wicker baskets hang from their arms. Nearby a sun-browned field hand repairs a cedar rail fence, and a pair of Galloway oxen turn rich earth toward the sun. Some of the village's flock of sheep are grazing in a pasture.

You pause at the Half Way House and make inquiries about the stage coach. "Should be here 'bout any time now," you are told. Two travellers with carpet bags are waiting. One is going to Toronto to visit a relative. The other, an itinerant dentist, is on his way to Toronto to catch the steamboat to Cobourg.

You turn left onto Mill Road. The noise of children at play draws your attention to the little one-room schoolhouse. You stop and watch the games of hopscotch and blind-man's buff until the schoolmaster appears and rings the bell. Immediately the children cease their activities and disappear one by one into the schoolhouse, girls in one entrance, boys in the other. They have to get ready for a spelling bee and excitement runs high.

A wagon pulled by a team of draught horses passes you on its way to Roblin's Mill. The farmer waves a greeting as he drives by. The growing season has been good this year and he is taking a load of wheat to the mill to have it ground into flour.

The door of the broommaker's shop is open and you find him hard at work getting an order of new brooms ready for the Laskay Emporium. The broom corn he uses to make them was likely grown back of his house last year. He is a batchelor and his workshop also serves as his living quarters.

The cabinetmaker whose shop is located in the east wing of the carriage works has just finished turning some new chair legs on his foot-powered lathe for one of his customers.

Outside the blacksmith shop a farmer has led his ox up on the rack so that the smith can fit the animal with new shoes.

As you continue on your way from one building to another, you feel yourself losing sense of time and inevitably you succumb to the charms of this lively mid-19th century community.

Created by The Metropolitan Toronto and Region Conservation Authority in the early 1960s, Black Creek Village was planned to show the progress of an early Ontario community to the time of Confederation in 1867. The village consists of a variety of original 19th century buildings, carefully moved to the site, restored and authentically furnished to the period.

The nucleus of the village is made up of the farm buildings once owned by Daniel Stong, a Pennsylvania German settler. Standing on their original sites, they comprise Daniel's first simple log home built in 1816, his grain barn, piggery, and smokehouse which were added later, and the family's second more commodious house erected in 1832. Their pioneer farm tells the story of rural life in early Upper Canada, from the time the land on which the village now stands was first settled by Daniel and his new bride, the former Elizabeth Fisher, to the days when their growing family had begun to prosper and enjoy the fruits of their labour.

Daniel Stong was nine years old when he joined his mother, father, brother and sister in the 500-mile trek from Huntington County, Pennsylvania, to Vaughan Township in York County. In 1800, the family crossed the Niagara River at Black Rock to Fort Erie on a ferry, followed an Indian trail east to Toronto, and completed their journey north on Yonge Street, then a rough road hacked out of the bush.

The Stongs left Pennsylvania for a variety of reasons: high taxation, scarcity of arable land, and a promise from John Graves Simcoe, the Lieutenant-Governor of Upper Canada, that north of the border they would obtain ample land for farming. Simcoe knew that the key to the future of Upper Canada lay in colonizing the vast expanse of this as yet sparsely settled land. The source of new colonists, he believed, was to be found in the United States where a large number of people, loyal to the British Crown, had remained after the Revolutionary War rather than joining the exodus of Loyalists to Upper Canada. Many of these former subjects of the King, Simcoe was convinced, would now prefer to live again under British rule.

In his proclamation of February 7, 1792, he offered land grants of up to 1,000 acres in Upper Canada to prospective settlers who would give assurance that they would cultivate and improve their grants and take an oath of loyalty to King George III of England.

In response to Simcoe's call, a large exodus of emigrants from the United States began around 1796. Their peaceful invasion of Upper Canada resulted in the settlement of many of the vacant townships north of Lake Ontario. By 1805, approximately 4,000 Pennsylvania Germans had settled in Markham, Vaughan, York, Pickering, Scarborough and Whitchurch townships of York County, and the townships of Waterloo County to the west. The Stong family was among them.

The Stong Settlement and Life on the Farm

Daniel Stong, who at the age of 20 had enlisted and seen service in the War of 1812, married Elizabeth in January of 1816. The bride from Vaughan Township was the daughter of John and Catherine Hommen Fisher, and the newlyweds began their life together on lot 25, Conc. 4 in West York, a tract of wilderness Elizabeth had inherited.

Like all the pioneers who came to Upper Canada to establish a farm, Daniel had to start by clearing some land to erect a shelter. The forest was a daunting obstacle. During the fall it was beautiful when the hues and colours of the trees mixed together to produce an effect equal in the words of one early observer to that of "a tropical forest in spring, when covered with blossoms." Yet it was intimidating and the enormous pines, oaks and maples which had never felt the woodsman's axe dwarfed a grown man and depressed his spirits.

Daniel and Elizabeth, however, had youth and the enthusiasm and hopes of newlyweds in their favour. They rolled up their sleeves and tackled the work at hand.

The trees Daniel cut on his land provided the building material for the couple's first home, a simple structure of squared logs, about 12 by 20 feet. The corners were dovetailed, reinforcing the tight fit of the squared logs so that little chinking with moss or clay was needed between the spaces.

Daniel Stong's first house is built of squared logs. The corners are dovetailed to assure a tight fit.

The roofs of pioneer homes as a rule were covered with handmade shingles of split pine, cedar or spruce. Some had roofs made of hollowed basswood logs semi-circular in shape and laid like tile, hollow side up alternating with hollow side down. Often the door was merely an opening over which a blanket was hung. Windows in early cabins were rare. Glass was expensive and difficult to obtain. Sometimes oiled paper was laid over a hole cut out of the logs to admit some light. Writer Susanna Moodie, herself an immigrant to Upper Canada, regarded such early settlers' cabins as "dens of misery which would be shamed by an English pigsty."

The Stong's first house, while primitive by a genteel Englishwoman's standards, was well built and functional, a reflection of the sturdy pioneer who had built it.

No space is wasted. The house consists of three rooms, the largest being the kitchen where Elizabeth prepared and cooked the meals on the open hearth and where all of the family's activities were carried out. The two smaller rooms at the rear were bedrooms.

As there was a sawmill nearby, the floor of the Stong Home was made of heavy pine planks, kept clean by Elizabeth using a fine sand mixed with lye. Her broom was fashioned from hemlock or cedar boughs tied to a handle.

Seven of Daniel and Elizabeth's eight children were born in the house. The baby's cradle was always kept in the parents' room while the older children occupied the second bedroom or slept on the floor in front of the fireplace in the kitchen.

The Stong family's first house, built in 1816.

The all-important fireplace served for cooking and heating and as a gathering place for the family on cold winter evenings. Canniff Haight in his book, *Country Life in Canada*, describes such a scene at the fireplace

> around which gathered in the winter time bright and happy faces; where the old men smoked their pipes in peaceful reverie, or delighted us with stories of other days; where mother darned her socks, and father mended our boots; where the girls were sewing, and uncles were scraping axe-handles with bits of glass to make them smooth.

At a time when matches were non-existent, one had to be vigilant that the fire never went out. When it did happen, someone would have to be sent to the neighbours a half-mile away, or more, to fetch some live coals.

Two iron rings set in one side of the fireplace support a crane, fitted with a trammel for kettles and pots which can be swung over and away from the fire.

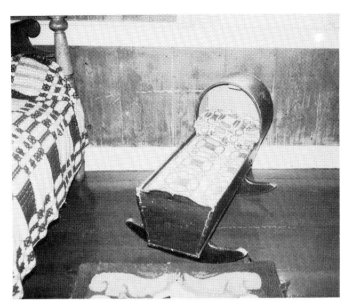

The parents' bedroom with the baby's cradle in the second Stong house.

The fireplace with cooking utensils in the kitchen of the first Stong house.

Iron pots and kettles used by the pioneers came in various shapes and sizes for baking, broiling or frying. Utensils such as the spider, a frying pan with three legs, the saucepan, the gridiron and the toasting fork all had long handles so they could be taken out of the fire. The spit was used for rendering bacon or roasting small birds and the dripping fat was saved to make candles or soap.

Herbs, grown by most settlers for use in cooking or for medicinal purposes, were hung from the ceiling to dry over the fireplace. Apple slices or bits of pumpkin too were dried close to the heat to preserve them for winter.

Near his house, Daniel Stong built a piggery to shelter his hogs. As salt pork was the settlers' main source of meat, smokehouses in farmyards were a common site in Upper Canada. The Stongs' smokehouse where their meat was cured was put to good use for many years. The pork had to be soaked in brine for six to eight weeks before being hung on hooks from the ceiling while a fire of hickory, green maple or dry corncobs slowly burned in a large iron kettle, providing the smudge for the smoke which gave a peculiar flavour to the hams and acted as a preservative for the meat.

* * *

Clearing the land in order to raise his crops was a tedious process for the settler. His best helpers were a pair of oxen, indispensable on a pioneer farm as they were better suited than horses for brushing, logging, hauling, removing stumps, and ploughing over rough ground. Oxen were not as likely to sink in mud or snow as horses. When it happened, they would flop on their bellies and wait patiently to be rescued, whereas horses tended to thrash about and by so doing, endangered themselves and their owner. Although a pair of good oxen might cost a settler $75.00, a large sum of money in those days, their upkeep was cheap. They could be fed on rough hay and marsh grass which was available in abundance. Working horses, on the other hand, needed better quality hay and grain for feed. An expensive harness was a necessity for a team of horses but a pair of oxen needed nothing more than a homemade yoke.

A pair of oxen pulling stumps.

When the trees had been felled the trunks were burned along with the brush. One burning was often inadequate and the partially-burnt brush had to be gathered up and the fire started up again. At the end of the day the men were as black as chimney sweeps. The ash that was left after burning hardwood trees provided an excellent source of potash which the settler was able to sell for ready cash or use as barter at the nearest general store for things he could not make himself.

By the 1850s much of the good farmland in Upper Canada had been brought under cultivation. Tasks to which the oxen had been so well adapted—brushing, logging, stumping—were no longer needed. Agricultural implements had been greatly improved and horses were more practical on a developed farm. Good mares were being imported from Britain and stallions from New England and the breeding of the two produced a superior work animal. Thus, the horse gradually replaced the ox.

Now the horse was used for ploughing and hauling and taking the family to church on Sunday. Yet the farmer did not easily forget the beast that helped him clear the land in the difficult beginning years, and an old, worn oxen yoke could still be found hanging in most grain barns for years to come.

The oxen kept at Black Creek Village are reminders of the important role these strong and dependable animals played in clearing the Upper Canadian wilderness.

* * *

Although settlers now were able to raise a variety of crops, wheat remained the staple in Upper Canada and was an important export commodity. Oats, barley and rye were grown as cattle feed and part of the barley and rye crop was sold to distilleries. The first field crops were sown by hand, the sower scattering the seeds with a sweeping motion of the arm as he walked across the field.

By the 1830s the Toronto Nursery on Dundas Street offered over 80 varieties of apple trees for sale. Daniel Stong selected some fine specimens for his apple orchard and some of the trees he planted survived well into the 20th century.

Leicester sheep at Black Creek Village provide wool for weaving.

A cedar rail fence enclosing an orchard.

For their wool supply settlers kept a flock of sheep like the Leicester, a breed known for their long white fleece suitable for providing the warm clothing and blankets needed in the cold winters of Upper Canada. Shearing was carried out in late spring, usually the first week in June, the sheep having first been taken to a stream or lake and washed. Sometimes a tobacco solution had to be applied to get rid of vermin.

Cleaning, sorting and carding the wool was women's work as was the spinning and weaving of the family's clothes and blankets. Girls learned these tasks from their mothers at an early age. As soon as they were able they were expected to do their share of the work. There was no time for idleness in the household of a pioneer settler. Commonly used was the large spinning wheel which required the spinner to walk back and forth whirling the wheel with one hand, drawing the wool into yarn and guiding the wool on the spindle with the other hand.

> The merry song of the girls, mingling with the hum of the spinning wheel, as they tripped backward and forward to the cadence of their music, drawing out the miles of thread, reeling it into skeins, which the weaver's loom and shuttle was to turn into thick heavy cloth; or old grandmother treading away at her little wheel, making it buzz as she drew out the delicate fibres of flax, and let it run up with the spindle a fine and evenly twisted thread, with which to sew our garments, or to make our linen; and mother, busy as a bee, thinking of us all, and never wearying in her endeavours to add to our comfort—these are the pictures that stand out, clear and distinct.
>
> Canniff Haight: *Country Life in Canada*

From "The Pioneers of Old Ontario"

Spinning Flax

The small spinning wheel with its foot-operated treadle allowed the spinner to sit. Immigrants from Europe often brought this type of spinning wheel with them to Upper Canada. Fitted with a distaff, it could be used for spinning flax.

Flax was grown by most settlers to provide linen thread for clothing and linens. In late summer, before the seeds were ripe, the plants were pulled up by hand, and when the sheaves had dried the seed balls were removed by combing or rippling. Afterwards the flax was taken to a nearby pond where it was weighted down with stones and kept under water for two or three weeks until the stems split open. Spread out and dried in the sun after the retting process was completed, the flexible inner part could be loosened by pounding the woody stalks between a flax brake. Then the fibres were drawn through a hatchel to separate broken fibres from the good ones. The former were spun into rope or used to make coarse cloth for straw ticks or sacking. The smooth silky fibres meanwhile were arranged on the distaff of the spinning wheel and spun into fine linen thread.

* * *

In 1825 Daniel built a grain barn on his property. As was the custom in those days, he no doubt asked his friends and neighbours to come to a barn raising bee. Bees were an excellent and agreeable way of sharing the work load. If the men had logging and barn raising bees, the women held quilting bees and the younger folk had fun at corn husking and apple peeling bees.

Daniel Stong's grain barn, built in 1825.

In the case of a barn raising, excitement ran high. If it was a large barn, up to a hundred men would be needed. On "raising day," under the direction of a master carpenter, they were divided into two gangs, each with an experienced captain, to speed up the work and get a race going to see which group would have their job done first. The heavy timbers had already been placed on the foundation and sleepers laid across. With long poles the men pushed up the upright timbers known as "bents", that made up the frame. After all the bents had been raised, timber "plates" on which rafters would rest were placed on top of the posts, one on each side of the barn. The timbers were fastened with wooden pins driven into place with wooden mallets. Canniff Haight recollects the scene from his youth:

> The noise of the men shouting and driving in the wooden pins with great wooden beetles, away up in the beams and stringers, alarmed me a great deal, but it all went up, and then one of the men mounted the plate (the timber on which the foot of the rafter rests) with a bottle in his hand, and swinging it round his head three times, threw it off into the field. If the bottle was unbroken it was an omen of good luck.

If all went well, the work was done by evening.

For days prior to a barn raising, the housewife with the help of her friends would be busy preparing for the supper she was expected to provide for the men. Their families usually were invited as well to the feast. Makeshift tables set up outside groaned under the sumptuous food and drink. A dance on the floor of the new barn marked the end of the day.

Daniel Stong's grain barn has two large hay or grain mows and a double threshing floor. The agricultural implements that were kept in the barn included a flail, a grain cradle, a harrow and ploughs. Wheat, flax and peas were stored in the granary.

The Dalziel barn on the grounds of Black Creek Village is another example of an early Pennsylvania German barn. Solid and well weathered, this large barn was erected on the site in 1809 to house livestock and store feed and wheat. Like the Stong barn it has a large threshing floor.

*   *   *

Before the threshing machine made its appearance in Upper Canada, grain was threshed with a flail, a hand threshing implement consisting of a wooden handle at the end of which a shorter stick was hung by a leather thong so as to swing freely. Swinging the flail over his head, the farmer would strike the wheat sheaves on the barn floor to separate the grain.

23

From "The Pioneers of Old Ontario"
Winnowing Grain

that they were evenly trampled. The process separated the grain which was then swept into a pile. Four horses could thus trod out thirty bushels of grain in a day.

Throughout the winter, the floor of the grain barn would vibrate with the regular thump, thump of the flails or the trampling of the animals' feet.

Finally, the chaff had to be separated from the wheat kernels which was done by winnowing. On a windy day the barn doors were opened to create a draft and the grain, placed in a large basket or on a wooden tray, was shaken so that the chaff which was lighter than the kernels was carried away by the wind. Sometimes a blanket was used in the winnowing, and two women would toss the grain into the air. As they did, the chaff would be blown away. The straw was used as bedding for the livestock and the cleaned grain was stored in the granary until it could be taken to the mill to be ground into flour.

In the fall the barn floor might be the scene of a husking bee. Tin lanterns with candles inside provided the light as the young people invited to the bee gathered in early evening. Boys and girls were sitting together, husking the corn which had been piled up on one side of the barn. Husks stripped off the ears were kept to stuff mattresses, while the cobs, stripped of their kernels, were thrown in piles in the centre, perhaps to be used later to keep the fire burning in the smokehouse when the time came to cure the meat after the "killing." A boy finding a coloured cob was rewarded with a kiss from the girl of his choice. An innocent "kissing game" such as this was an acceptable substitute for dancing which by some of the elders was frowned upon.

One man could thresh between eight and twelve bushels in a day, a good thresher making it up to fifteen. If he was a hired man, he would receive one-tenth of what he had threshed in addition to his board.

Sometimes the threshing was done with the help of animals. A layer of sheaves was spread on the barn floor. Oxen or horses were driven to walk around in a circle, while a man kept turning the sheaves so

Diversions were few in number in those early days of settlement, and social gatherings such as a bee to share the work at hand did much to lessen the hardships of pioneer life and the feeling of isolation at a time when farms were spread far apart.

* * *

If a farmer's workday was long and hard, so was that of the farmer's wife. The old saying "a woman's work is never done" was certainly true in her case. Although in time she was able to enjoy a few labour-saving devices, her chores were never ending.

There were candles to be made from the fat saved after an animal had been slaughtered. Spun linen thread was twisted into a wick and dipped repeatedly in the liquid tallow to build up a thick candle. If she had a mould she was able to cast a few candles at once.

The cream skimmed off the family cow's milk had to be churned into butter once or twice a week. The laborious job of churning, requiring a steady up and down agitation of the wooden dasher, was carried out by younger members of the family. When the cream finally was separating into butter and buttermilk, the former was removed from the churn to a wooden bowl and washed a few times in cold water to remove all traces of the buttermilk. Excess water was then squeezed out by "working" the butter with wooden paddles. The buttermilk was used for baking or enjoyed by the family as a cooling drink.

Cheese for the family's consumption was made from the small extra supply of milk. A special cheese made from sour milk was introduced in Upper Canada by the Pennsylvania Germans. Known as "schmier kase," it was made by scalding sour milk that had thickened. The solid part which separated from the whey was wrapped in cloth and hung up to drain.

Nothing was wasted on the pioneer farm. Scraps of pork, rinds and fat were thrown into a barrel and when enough had accumulated the housewife made a batch of soap. Adding lye that had been leached from hardwood ashes she boiled it with the grease in a large iron kettle hung over a brisk fire built outside. Sometimes a bit of turpentine or resin was added during the boiling process to improve the quality of the soap. One barrel of ashes to twelve pounds of grease made about 40 pounds of soft soap.

From "The Pioneers of Old Ontario"
Soap-making in the early days

Hard soap was made from soft soap by adding a few handfuls of salt to the boiling mixture, then leaving it to set overnight before boiling it once again with some added turpentine and more salt. When the bubbling soap began to thicken, it was ready to be poured into moulds.

Soap was only made when the moon was new as superstition had it that it would be drying out if it were made when the moon was on the wane.

* * *

The Stong family's second house, built of hand-hewn timbers in 1832.

In 1832, sixteen years after first making a clearing in the bush, Daniel Stong constructed a fine two-storey seven-room house of hand-hewn timbers, some measuring 30 inches in diameter. Covered with clapboard siding, the house was built on a stone foundation. The roof consisted of planks nailed on top of the rafters and covered with wooden shingles. A verandah across the front added to the appearance of the house which reflected the measure of prosperity achieved by its owner. The exterior was painted reddish-brown, a favourite colour at the time, and in contrast to the majority of houses in Upper Canada in those days which never saw a coat of paint and over the years acquired a rustic grey appearance.

The only entrance to the house was the front door which opened into a large kitchen. Here the housewife's pride and joy was her large brick fireplace with its bake oven that was a marked improvement over her former facilities for cooking and baking.

A hardwood fire would be kindled in the built-in bake oven and kept burning until the wood was reduced to a white ash. The coals were then raked out and the bread, pies or other food placed in the oven with a long-handled paddle called a peel.

Bread appeared at all meals and baking bread was another of the housewife's many daily tasks. "The making and baking of good, nourishing, palatable bread is perhaps one of the most important duties of the practical housewife," wrote Catharine Parr Traill in her description of pioneer life. The dough was made up and put to rise in the dough box beside the fireplace at night. In the morning, after it was kneaded down, it was formed into loaves.

By the 1830s most homes of prosperous settlers would have a bake oven, located beside the fireplace, but in the early days the pioneers had to make do with iron bake kettles. Hot coals were placed on top and below the kettle which had to be rotated regularly to ensure even baking during the forty minutes required to bake the bread.

The reflector oven, an oblong box of bright tin with a slanting top and open on one side which came next, was a great improvement. Placed on the hearth, its open side faced the fire. Inside, the tins containing the dough were lifted slightly to allow the heat to circulate.

The cast-iron cooking stove introduced in the 1830s, although it was a labour-saving and efficient appliance for cooking, was expensive and often inadequate when preparing food for a large family. Women of the older generation had grown set in their ways and were not easily persuaded to give up their methods of cooking that had proved tried and true.

Preparing the meals for her family and the hired help was a matter of great importance for a farmer's wife. A hearty fare was essential for the workers whose day began before sunup and ended at sundown. Food on the table of a farm kitchen was expected to be plentiful and good.

A variety of fruits was grown in Upper Canada and berries, plums, grapes and cherries were turned into preserves and stored in earthen crocks. Apples from the farm orchard figured prominently in the settlers' diet and were eaten in a number of ways including steamed apple dumplings, apple pie, apple sauce and apple butter. Some apples were dried for use in winter or pressed in the cider mill and kept for drinking purposes at bees and other social gatherings. Left exposed to air, some of the cider became vinegar used for cooking.

A specialty of the Pennsylvania Germans was sauerkraut. Elizabeth Stong would make it the way she had been taught by her mother, by placing alternating layers of shredded cabbage and salt in a large barrel or crock. When the barrel was filled, the cabbage was stomped with a wooden stomper and weighted down with heavy stones placed on a board. After a while the contents fermented and the "sour" cabbage was ready to eat. Some referred to it as "rotten cabbage," but the German settlers consumed large quantities of the sauerkraut during the winter months, when fresh vegetables were not available.

* * *

Just how much the Stong family's lifestyle had improved since they first settled on their land is evident from the finer furnishings and amenities in their second home. There are handwoven blinds and curtains and small handmade rugs which provide a spot of colour.

The parlour with its tongue and groove pine paneling, its writing desk, couch, rocking chairs and a box stove imported from Scotland speaks of growing prosperity. In those days the parlour was the formal room of the house and was used only on special occasions, such as the minister's visit or a family celebration. As a rule the room was kept in darkness to prevent the upholstery and wallpaper from fading.

Instead of a painting a framed sampler would sometimes decorate the wall. Made of coarse canvas cloth and embroidered in various stitches with letters or a verse from the Bible, samplers were an example of a young lady's skills.

The dulcimer, a wire-stringed instrument played with light hammers, might be found in some of the settlers' homes by the 1830s, an indication that there now was some time for leisure.

Daniel and Elizabeth Stong and their youngest

child slept in a bedroom off the parlour on the main floor where they were closest to the fire and could hear the call of alarmed livestock or the knock of a traveller seeking shelter for the night. Upstairs were the bedrooms of the older children. The girls' bedroom was directly above that of their parents and could be reached from there by a narrow stairway. The simple furnishings of the room included dowry pieces consisting of a table, a chair, a bed and chest and a clothes press. The boys of the family shared a large bedroom.

Handmade coverlets on the beds indicate that Elizabeth and her daughters were able to devote some hours of their day to the finer things in life. Quilting bees were a pleasant way of socializing and gossiping with neighbours and friends while producing with their help a pretty patchwork quilt from scraps of worn clothing. Canniff Haight describes such a quilting bee:

> when the women and girls of the neighourhood assembled in the afternoon, and turned out those skilfully and often artistically made rugs, so comfortable to lie under during the cold winter nights. There was often a great deal of sport at the close of one of these social industrial gatherings. When the men came in from the field to supper, some luckless wight was sure to be caught and tossed up and down in the quilt amid the laughter and shouts of the company.

Quilting was a craft taught to the daughters of the family at an early age, and every girl would have a number of quilts in her hope chest by the time she was engaged to be married. Then friends and neighbours were invited to help complete the special quilt which would adorn the young couple's marriage bed.

The kitchen garden behind the house was Elizabeth's domain. Potatoes, corn, squash, beans, cabbage, turnips and onions were commonly grown in a 19th century garden. A typical Pennsylvania German garden such as that of the Stongs was planted in square beds edged by boards and separated by narrow walks. Herbs were grown for culinary as well as medicinal purposes and the plot was enclosed by a board fence to keep out rooting animals. In the fall some vegetables would be stored in a root cellar or pickled in homemade vinegar. Herbs were carefully gathered to be dried for use in winter.

The Gristmill

By mid-19th century even a small village which had grown around an early crossroads farm such as that of the Stongs had many of the amenities which come with orderly development. Roads were linking communities providing better access to markets. Craftsmen had long since established shops and were plying trades which satisfied the needs of inhabitants. Whatever else the heart desired could probably be obtained in the general store, if not for money, then by bartering one's produce or in exchange for labour. There was a schoolhouse and at least one church built with the sacrifice of a dedicated congregation.

A view of Roblin's Gristmill with its large wooden waterwheel.

The owner of the local gristmill by all accounts was a fairly prosperous man. Gristmills had been built on most of the suitable water sites in Upper Canada, and many a now-bustling community had formed around an early mill. Time was when a farmer had to grind his grain himself using a quern, which was a type of handmill, or he had to travel by foot or wagon for many miles to have his flour milled at the nearest mill. A new mill was a boon to settlement, and attracted in turn other industries that assured the community's self-sufficiency. Waterpower was needed to run the machinery of a mill in the days before steam power was harnessed for that purpose and settlements followed a pattern shaped by the courses of rivers and streams.

The imposing five-storey stone mill with its 18.5 foot wooden waterwheel at Black Creek Village is typical of the many mills dotting the waterways of Upper Canada in the 19th century.

Roblin's Mill traces its origin back to 1842 when Owen Roblin, grandson of a United Empire Loyalist, erected the mill at Ameliasburg, Prince Edward County. His mill had a capacity of 100 barrels of flour a day and was in operation twenty-four hours a day when water levels permitted. Much of the mill's output, packed in barrels made in Roblin's own cooperage, was transported to the nearest port and loaded on steamers for shipment to Montreal or the United States. Competition from mills in larger centres with access to rail transportation forced the Roblin mill to close in 1920.

Taken down piece by piece in the early 1960s, the mill was reconstructed at Black Creek Pioneer Village where its huge waterwheel operates two runs of stones, milling flour as in Owen Roblin's time.

Early waterwheels came in various types and

sizes. If a mill was located at the base of a waterfall, it was run by an undershot wheel which derived its power by the force of the rushing water striking its blades. The overshot wheel requiring a mill dam, pond and water control system was still common in Upper Canada when Roblin built his mill. Later with advances in mill technology came the water turbine which eventually replaced the wooden waterwheel and greatly improved a mill's efficiency.

At Black Creek Village the flow of water from the upper millpond is carefully regulated as it passes through a flume to the mill. Once Black Creek would have had sufficient water flow to keep a mill running throughout the summer. Today it is necessary to reuse the water after it has tumbled over the wheel, by pumping it back to the pond. The overshot wheel derives its power from the force of gravity as the water falls on top of the wheel filling its wooden buckets and causing it to turn. The wheel's axle is connected to belts and gears which operate the mill's machinery.

Wheat brought by the farmer for custom milling is weighed at the receiving door before being dropped into a hopper. It then goes down a chute to the bottom of an elevator which is an endless belt with a number of buckets that convey grain and flour from one floor to another. Carried to the top floor by the elevator, the grain is cleaned from foreign matter first in a revolving screen and then in a smutter, a drum, covered by a screen, revolving at high speed. From a holding bin, the clean wheat moves to the stones for milling it into flour, which the farmer will take home to his wife for her to bake the bread. At Roblin's Mill one run of stones is used to do such custom milling.

Millstones usually were made from French burr-stone, a superior hard quartz from a region near Paris which takes and holds a sharp edge. Poured slowly into the eye of the stones, the grain is ground moving through the furrows cut in the stones, the top stone known as the "runner" revolving while the "bedstone" at the bottom remains stationary. As the quality of the flour depends on the sharpness of the furrows, the stones have to be frequently "dressed" by the millwright who with picks must carefully recut the dulled edges, a tedious job requiring time and skill.

From the stones, the flour goes down a chute to the bucket elevator which moves it to the bolting reel where it passes through a screen to sift the flour.

A second pair of stones at Roblin's Mill is used for milling commercial flour, such as would have been required to ship in barrels to towns and cities across the country or to be exported. After the milling process, commercial flour is cooled, then refined in the bolting chest which consists of several reels with different gauges of screening and produces superfine white flour, and depending on the coarseness of the screen, second grade flour, middlings, bran and at the end "shorts" which could be sold as feed for pigs.

By law the miller was entitled to retain one twelfth of the farmer's wheat in payment for his services.

Other Early Industries and Crafts

If the miller was an important man in a developing community, so was the local blacksmith. He was called upon to supply all the wrought ironware needed by the settlers. He could make nails and fireside tools and other essential cooking ware, mend a harrow or a plough, iron a whippletree while the farmer waited, or make new shoes for a man's horses and oxen. He forged hinges, tools, hasps, perhaps a new trammel for the crane at the fireplace or a decorative wrought iron work ordered by a customer. If the machinery at the mill needed repair, the blacksmith was the one to call on. In an age when horses and wagons or, in winter, cutters were the mode of transportation, the blacksmith often was a wheelwright as well. Rough and bumpy corduroy roads quickly wore down the iron tires on the wooden wheels of a vehicle and the traveller had to stop at a smithy to have them repaired.

The blacksmith shop at Black Creek Village, a small building of board and batten construction, dates back to the late 1850s and comes from Nobleton, Ontario. The focus of the smithy is its forge kept crackling with the aid of oxhide bellows which work like a large lung and by expansion and contraction draw in air through an orifice and expel it through a rod onto the charcoal in the grate. An apprentice may have worked the arm attached to the bellows while the smith, using tongs, held the glowing metal in the fire. Pulling it out of the fire when the iron turned white, he would hammer and shape the metal on his anvil.

Today the blacksmith at Black Creek repairs and restores the implements and carriages of the inhabitants and sees to it that the fourteen horses—Clydesdales, one "Canadian" and a few other draught horses—are properly shod. The pair of Galloway belted oxen which do their share of work in the village require special shoes to fit their cloven hooves.

* * *

From "The Pioneers of Old Ontario"
Pit-Saw

A custom sawmill was among the early industries in most developing settlements. Wood was plentiful and settlers needed building material. Most of these sawmills were waterpowered, and being located close to the water's edge, they received their supply of logs during the annual riverdrive in the spring.

From the 1860s on, however, when railways were beginning to spread their iron bands across the province, dependence on waterways for transportation diminished and steam powered sawmills could be found in some locations removed from streams or rivers.

The sawmill now being restored at Black Creek Pioneer Village is one of these steam powered mills which were able to supply sawn lumber to their customers on a year-round basis. Next door to the mill is the sawyer's house. A sawyer would not likely have been among the well-to-do in the village, but he would have been able to live comfortably.

* * *

The harness shop and saddlery at the Village is the shop of a highly skilled artisan who must possess a thorough knowledge of the properties of leather. Occasionally a harnessmaker may also have been a tanner, making his own supply of leather.

Articles fashioned by the harnessmaker include saddlery gear, leather aprons such as are worn by the blacksmith, leather trunks and bags for the travelling public, belts and horse collars stuffed with straw and shaped to fit the animal's neck. Threads for stitching are prepared each day by rolling together strands of hemp and treating them with beeswax and pitch from a pine tree to make them pliable and waterproof. His fine handcrafted leather articles are preserved by rubbing the leather with a cloth dipped in oil.

* * *

The Harness Shop and Saddlery.

Dominion Carriage Works, 1867, with the cabinetmaker's shop located in the east wing.

Housed in the east wing of the former carriage works at Black Creek Village is the cabinetmaker's shop.

While a few wealthy early settlers could afford to bring furniture pieces from overseas or the United States with them to Upper Canada, the majority of people arriving as refugees from the aftermath of the American Revolution or with the waves of later immigrants were forced to make their own simple and often crude furniture. Cabinetmakers as such were few and far between in Upper Canada in the beginning, but by the middle of the 19th century most villages could boast at least one cabinetmaker.

Working with a foot-powered lathe and jigsaw and a variety of other tools, the cabinetmaker made at first functional, plain-looking cupboards, chairs and tables. He repaired spinning wheels, made window frames and interior trim. His stock-in-trade included cradles, bedsteads, washstands and candle stands.

By mid-century, he had adapted new skills and techniques to meet the growing demands of his clients. He watched the mixing of preferences and designs from England, the border States, and Europe.

Often his furniture is heavier, more ornate with clawed feet or fancy scrollwork along the edges. His cabinet drawers are finely dovetailed. The finishing could be varied and decorative. On pine wood he could simulate walnut grain, or birds-eye maple. He might paint his pieces with effective red, yellow and blue-green combinations. On dowry boxes he may paint natural scenes, of birds and woodlands; or on a kitchen table he will try his hand at fancy stencils which the Germans and Dutch love so much.

One item he was frequently called on to make was a coffin and consequently he came to be the village undertaker.

The building occupied by the cabinetmaker stood in the Stratford area prior to being moved to Black Creek Village. It served as a blacksmith and wheelwright shop before their enterprises were converted into the Dominion Carriage Works during the 1860s. A mid-sized carriage works, the company manufactured and repaired carriages and wagons, and was equipped with a trim shop, paint and varnish rooms, forges and a carpenter's shop and employed a blacksmith, cabinetmaker, upholsterer and a wheelwright among its skilled craftsmen.

* * *

Another highly-skilled artisan at Black Creek Village is the gunsmith. The building where he has set up shop came from Bolton, Ontario.

Early settlers who depended on wild meat to supplement their diet of pork on occasion needed the services of a gunsmith. Not only did he repair old guns, many of which were imported weapons used by the militia, but he would also assemble new firearms for his customers.

A gunsmith, perhaps more than any other craftsman, has to be a multi-talented person. Apprenticed to a master, he needs up to seven years to learn his craft. To make a gun requires working with wood and metal, hence he has to become proficient as a cabinetmaker as well as a blacksmith. Since fine metal is involved also, he has to learn the skills of a silversmith and to make a gun's intricate mechanism function, he has to be an accomplished locksmith.

His support comes primarily from the wealthier class of residents. The cost of a finely crafted gun took nearly a working man's yearly wage, but in an early society where able-bodied men required a gun to protect their livestock or to procure game for the table, the gunsmith was never short of requests for his services.

* * *

One industry of the 1800s which enjoyed a steady demand for its products was the cooperage. The cooper made nearly all the types of containers needed in those days, including barrels, buckets and tubs, and he would find a ready market for his craft. Barrels were used for packing and transporting a wide variety of goods such as grain, flour, apples, cider, even nails, and at the general store molasses, sugar and whiskey were always stored in barrels.

The Taylor Cooperage at Black Creek Village dates back to the 1850s when the owner started to manufacture barrels at Paris, Ontario.

* * *

The broommaker's shop at Black Creek is located in a one-room log house of the 1840s which also serves as his living quarters. Although a broommaker would sell his brooms quite readily to the local general store or directly to area farmers, he could at best make only a modest living selling his brooms wholesale at 25 cents each. The furnishings in his house are basic—a cookstove, a dry sink, cupboard, table and chairs, and a folding bed, along with his broommaking machine. His harvest of broom corn which was grown at the back of the house is stored in the attic.

Before they could obtain corn brooms the pioneers made birch brooms and splint brooms. Broom corn, an annual grass resembling Indian corn, was eventually imported from the New England states but by the 1850s it was also grown extensively in Canada West, as Upper Canada came to be called, and broommaking then became one of the cottage industries that could be found in many villages.

* * *

On the ground floor of the Masonic building at Black Creek we find the tinsmith at work in his shop which looks a bit like a hardware store.

At the tinsmith shop villagers could find every conceivable kind of tinware: plates, cups, candlesticks, washtubs and pitchers, in short household utensils of every description. Tin was relatively cheap and therefore made use of wherever possible. If the tinsmith's wife or one of his daughters were artistically inclined, they would perhaps paint some of the trays or jugs he had made to produce toleware which would fetch a higher price.

When cooking and heating stoves began to supplant the fireplace in settlers' homes, the local tinsmith was kept busy producing stove pipes for his customers.

Masonic Building.
The Tinsmith Shop is located on the ground floor.

The building in which the tinsmith shop is located dates back to the 1860s and was donated and restored by the Masons of Ontario under the direction of the Heritage Lodge as an example of the typical Masonic meeting place built in many early small towns of Ontario. The Masonic Lodge upstairs is fully furnished and is staffed by volunteer members of the Masonic Order.

* * *

The weaver's shop at Black Creek Village occupies part of a former Temperance Hall, built in 1850 by the Sons of Temperance in Kettleby, Ontario.

Professional weavers arriving as immigrants in Upper Canada were a boon to small communities. Producing yard goods from the wool or flax spun and dyed by the housewife, they freed her from the task of having to weave all her own household linens, blankets and materials for clothing. Some of the early weavers were itinerants, but as their reputation and their business grew they established shops in their communities, sometimes hiring spinning girls to prepare the wool or flax for weaving and thus offering a full range of services.

Charles Irvine's Weavers Shop.

The weaver at the Village has a "flying shuttle" loom, which is equipped with a mechanism that allows him to flick the shuttle back and forth and thus speed up production.

Outside his premises he maintains a "dye garden." The plants grown there allow him to produce dyes for fleece, yarn or fabric according to his customers' wishes. Among the plants are Solomon's seal and tansy used for shades of green; calendula, St.-John's-wort and coreopsis used for yellow; and bloodroot which creates red and orange colours. By the mid-1800s a variety of chemical dyes was also available.

Small weaver's shops like that at Black Creek were busy with custom work including the weaving of rag rugs on carpet looms, but with the advent of power looms and the emergence of woollen mills which employed the factory system of textile production, these weavers faced serious competition and their business declined.

* * *

Located in the north wing of the old Temperance Hall is the Black Creek Village Printing Office. Equipped with a working Washington flat bed press from the 1820s and a foot-powered Gordon press, it is typical of many such small 19th century print shops throughout Ontario which used to produce the local newspaper and print broadsides, political and religious tracts, advertisements and announcements for auction sales, church picnics and socials.

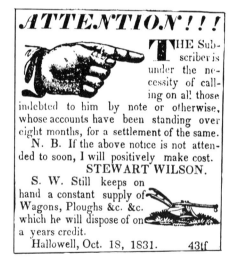

Local items could be found on the back pages. The gathering of foreign news was a slow and tedious job in the days before the telegraph, and news from the Old Country, arriving with transatlantic steamers, was often gleaned from American papers. Although the news was several weeks old by the time it reached the reader in Upper Canada, it was eagerly sought, and it re-enforced the ties many of the settlers still had with the land of their birth. Prior to the 1840s almost all of Ontario's papers were weeklies.

Frequently the owner of the paper was also the reporter, editor, typesetter and printer, running the shop with the help of a "printer's devil" who did the cleanup and made the ink from lampblack and varnish. The chase for printing had to be made up by hand from a supply of type and woodcuts.

Most printers were industrious, patriotic and law-abiding men, but their papers reflected their own political bias and thinking on the issues of the day. Hotly-debated topics in the era of organization and development of settlements included government patronage, corruption in high places, the handling of revenues from clergy reserves, and the greed of land speculators. Neither anti- nor pro-reform papers minced their words when espousing their respective causes. The fiery Scot, William Lyon Mackenzie, leader of the 1837 Rebellion in Upper Canada, ranted and raved against the powerful "Family Compact" rule of his day on the pages of his *Colonial Advocate*.

Inside the Black Creek Printing Office.

Early newspapers served to publicize government policies and give a voice to public opinion. The papers consisted of four pages with the second page as a rule devoted to editorials and readers' letters.

Many of these early papers were short-lived, their owners unable to cope with the financial risks the publishing business entailed. Money was scarce, and not everyone could afford a subscription which ranged between $3.00 and $5.00 a year. Most printers accepted rags, which were used in the manufacture of paper, as payment, but even then from time to time they had to remind subscribers to "pay or face the consequences." As a considerable number of settlers could not read, neighbours would gather in the evening on the day the paper came out to hear someone read the news and to spend a while debating matters of concern.

A milestone was reached in the printing industry in 1860 when paper began to be manufactured from wood pulp and printing costs due to cheaper newsprint were greatly reduced. Free education available to all was creating a continually rising demand for printed matter. Growing literacy in a rapidly expanding population translated into growing subscription lists. Mechanical inventions, such as the cylindrical and the rotary presses were speeding up production and newspapers could be issued daily.

* * *

As time went on, the apple orchards planted by the early pioneers matured and produced an overabundance of fruit. Apples were shipped in large quantities to markets, dried or kept in the cellar for home use in winter or made into cider and apple butter. Usually someone in the village had a cider mill and at harvest time cider-making bees would be held. Generally sour apples were used to make cider, sweet apples being added later for thickening when some of the cider was boiled down into syrup for making apple butter.

Early cider mills were crude contrivances. The process of milling was fairly simple and quite profitable.

The cider mill located at Black Creek Village is of 1840s vintage. It was built by Henry Snider at nearby Elia, an early Pennsylvania German settlement on the banks of Black Creek.

Equipped with a screw press, the mill can make about 500 gallons of cider a day. The apples are crushed in a grinder before being placed between layers of long rye or wheat straw in a large wooden box. The huge iron hand-operated screw press then squeezes out the juice which drips through the straw into a trough, the straw acting as a filter to eliminate impurities.

* * *

The Daniel Flynn Boot and Shoe Shop.

Daniel Flynn was a boot and shoemaker who would have learned his trade apprenticed to a master shoemaker for a number of years.

When striking out on his own, a shoemaker in the early days was likely to be itinerant, travelling from farm to farm with a case containing his tools and boarding with each family for the time it took to mend and make up a year's supply of new boots and shoes for each member. Later, he probably set up shop in a room of his own house, keeping patterns and lasts on the wall behind his cobbler's bench.

Flynn must have been well established in his community of Newtonbrook, Ontario, for in 1858 he was able to build a separate small shop adjacent to his house. The aroma of leather permeates the air in his shop, now located at Black Creek Village. There are all the tools of his trade, including various knives, needles, hammer, rubstick, beeswax, a lapstone on which to hammer the leather, bottles of blacking and a tub of water so he can soak and soften the leather.

The Homes of Some Villagers

Daniel Flynn's house, located next to his shop, is the typical home of a working class family in the Village. As an artisan who had a steady clientele and a reputation for quality work, Flynn was able to provide his family with some amenities most farmers in his day could not afford. His wife has a cook stove in her kitchen instead of a fireplace; she owns a sewing machine; and besides her vegetable garden, she also has a pretty flower garden indicating that she is able to spend some time on a hobby. The furniture is made of walnut; the fancy wallpaper is imported; quilts and coverlets on the beds are commercially rather than handmade and were probably bought on one of the family's trips into town.

* * *

Built in the 1840s, the Burwick House at Black Creek Village reflects the gracious way of living of a country gentleman, perhaps a retired army officer or a professional man. The house was moved to its present site in the early 1960s from Woodbridge (formerly known as Burwick), a few miles west of Black Creek.

The eight rooms in the house are furnished with exquisite pieces, many of them brought by the owner from the Old Country. The dining room displays the style of the Regency period, while Chippendale and Sheraton furniture are found in the parlour. Expensive wallpaper, Persian rugs and old-fashioned handwoven carpets add warmth and elegance. Fine English china graces the dining table and a beautiful grandfather clock chimes the hours.

In the bedrooms, the furniture of cherry and maple wood was probably made to order in the local cabinetmaker's shop as was the furniture in the kitchen. The open fireplace in the kitchen is used to do the cooking, while the baking is done in the brick oven located in the adjoining scullery.

At the rear of the house are the stables to accommodate a couple of horses, and the carriage house for the family's carriage and their cutter.

The grounds are still well-kept and fenced in. Residences of the well-to-do had a flower garden in front tended by the lady of the house, while the rest of the grounds were looked after by a hired hand.

The Burwick home.

* * *

The fireplace in the kitchen of the Burwick House.

The scullery adjoining the kitchen in the Burwick House.

Grandfather clock in the Burwick House.

Hanging cradle—Burwick House.

Sideboard in the dining room of the Doctor's House.

Once a community was well established it could expect to attract various professional people. A doctor taking up residence in a village and hanging out his shingle was a definite sign that the settlement was coming of age, and the presence of a doctor's office gave the inhabitants an added sense of security and permanence.

Hitherto, in case of sickness, they often had to rely on their own resources as the nearest doctor was likely to be miles away. From the Natives, the settlers learned about the healing properties of leaves, flowers, roots and tree barks, and recipes for effective herbal potions and other remedies for common illnesses—fever, diarrhoea, ague—were passed on from one generation to the next.

The Doctor's House, 1867

On the whole the people were strong and in good health thanks to their steady outdoor work, but in time of life-threatening epidemics such as cholera, smallpox or diphtheria which on occasion ravaged an entire township, a doctor was a godsend, and next to the minister he was probably the most important person in the community.

He delivered babies, removed an abscessed tooth or set a fractured bone and treated many of his patients' ailments with the time-honoured method of using leeches to cleanse their blood. He did very little in the line of surgery, other than amputate limbs perhaps crushed in a farm accident, a procedure which he had to perform in a matter of minutes, without the benefits of anesthesia other than a shot of strong whiskey. His patients were not only the people in his village, but also the families in the surrounding countryside. Often he was called out in the middle of the night to see to a sick child or do what he could for an old man dying from consumption. It would not have been unusual for him to have to stay all night at a patient's bedside.

The doctor's house at Black Creek Village was once a farmhouse. It was built in the 1830s by William James, a farmer in the Brampton area. Moved to the Village in the 1970s, the house was restored and furnished to become the village doctor's residence and office. The doctor's living quarters are located in one section of the house, while the other part with separate entrance serves as his office and the patients' waiting room.

The doctor is well off, although he has many patients who cannot afford to pay for his services in cash. Instead they might bring produce from their farm, or in the case of an artisan, pay him in the form of services or labour.

Being a batchelor, the doctor at Black Creek has a housekeeper. The kitchen with its double-level cook stove is her domain; above the kitchen are her living quarters. The rooms in the house, particularly the dining room, are furnished tastefully with fine pieces. The doctor's bedroom and den are located in the central part of the house. Another bedroom on the second floor above his office is used for visitors.

The grounds shaded by trees are well kept and the doctor's extensive medicinal garden contains his "natural pharmacy." Although the science of medicine was making rapid strides by 1867, the country doctor still relied on medicines made from the plants grown in his herb garden as a supplement to commercially available remedies for a variety of ailments.

The herb garden provides a wealth of plants for his medicinal remedies. These he is mixing himself after drying, measuring and crushing the plants. Many of his medical texts offer directions as did some popular tracts recommending standard recipes.

His patients might ask him about boiled rose petals for gargle and inflamed eyelids; or rose hip tea for increased energy. Crushed garlic worked wonders for asthma and colds, did it not? And soapwort took away the itch of poison ivy.

He could buy Peruvian bark, from the chinchona tree, which remained the one universal and effective remedy for years. Doctors knew of its worth, but nothing of the active healing ingredient, alkaloid quinine.

Up to and long beyond the time of Confederation quackery was a problem in Canada. Many quacks brought untold suffering to the sick, especially children. Their remedies contained harmful elements: mercury, laudanum, zinc and charcoal powders.

Documents of the time show advertisements for patent medicines that were fraudulent or hazardous. Flavoured whiskey was often the medicinal element in liniments, ointments, bitters and syrups. Other "cure-alls" contained opium, heroin and morphine.

Most early doctors in Upper Canada were retired or decommissioned Army or Navy surgeons, who might have been trained in the medical schools of London, Edinburgh or Dublin.

As immigration to Upper Canada increased, so too did the number of civilian doctors. Demands grew for local training schools and gradually teaching schools were established in Montreal, Toronto and Kingston. Legislation aimed at eliminating quacks, unlicenced practitioners, malpractice, and improving general public health standards steadily raised the level of medicine in Upper Canada.

* * *

The Mackenzie House, at first a simple log cabin erected in the 1830s by a Pennsylvania settler at Woodbridge, Ontario, was enlarged twenty years later and is now a one-and-a-half storey board and batten dwelling. Its last owner and occupant was the settler's great-grandson, Major Addison Alexander Mackenzie.

The building was moved to Black Creek Village around 1974, and serves as the home of the village clockmaker and his wife who as the village seamstress helps to augment the family income.

Comfortably furnished to the 1867 period, when parlours were the showpiece of the house with their dark walnut pieces and horsehair-upholstered sofas, the place reflects the tastes of the mid-Victorian era.

Off the parlour is the clockmaker's workshop where he repairs heirloom clocks and watches brought to him by the villagers, while his wife sits on her 1860s model treadle sewing machine near the window in her kitchen, sewing a new Sunday dress for one of her neighbours or altering an old one that has gone out of style.

When her husband was a boy, clocks were very expensive and rare. People estimated time by the sun's passage. But fashions and demands change. From the 1840's American clockmakers mass-produced portable boxclocks for the parlour; and most people liked a grandfather clock if space permitted. European immigrants carried pocket watches—and all these timepieces eventually needed repair and replacement parts. The Village clockmaker was kept very busy.

The Laskay Emporium and Post Office

The general store in a 19th century village was in a sense the forerunner of today's department store. Here the people could find anything their hearts may have desired from hardware, china, glass, wall hangings, turpentine, tobacco and liniments to foodstuffs, yard goods, boots and bonnets. The store's shelves were laden with tins, boxes and jars; kettles, buckets and rope hung from the ceiling; barrels of whiskey, sugar and molasses along with bins of flour and boxes of soap cluttered the floor space. The scent of fresh fruit and dried prunes permeated the air, and mingled with the aroma of imported cigars.

The farmer would bring his produce—butter, cheese, eggs, grain—to the store and barter for things he or his wife could not make for themselves. The storekeeper in turn would take the produce to the city and trade it for tools, dishes, spices and all the

The gunsmith at work in his shop.

luxuries his customers expected to find in a well-stocked general store.

The Laskay Emporium and Post Office.

The storekeeper of the Laskay Emporium was in a position to carry a wide variety of imported goods, cottons, oysters, fine wines, for his store was located near Toronto where he had good opportunities to do his trading. A lot of bookkeeping work was involved to keep track of transactions at a time when barter was often used and currency was in short supply. A variety of coins of varying values, including Spanish, American and English money along with tokens issued by some banks and businessmen, were in circulation. Not until 1857 was an act passed that would eventually bring some order to the Canadian monetary system.

The storekeeper of the 1860s was usually a well-educated person, and he would be the logical choice for the position of postmaster when the community had matured enough to warrant its own post office. As some of his customers could not read or write, occasionally he would be asked to read their mail to them. Prior to 1851, when the first postage stamp—known to today's collectors as the 3 penny beaver—was issued in Canada, there were no postage stamps and the recipient of a letter was expected to pay the postage. There were no envelopes either; the piece of paper was simply folded and sealed with sealing wax. The mail was conveyed from place to place by stage, mail coach or steamship and from the latter part of the 1850s by railway. Newspapers from larger centres too would arrive by mail and the local printer would be able to copy items of interest into his weekly paper. There being no home mail delivery, villagers and the people from the surrounding countryside would have to come to the store to get their mail. The post office at the Laskay Emporium at Black Creek Village is fully functioning; it is located in the back of the store just as it was when Joseph Baldwin, a successful saw and woollen mill owner, first opened the store in 1856 at Laskay, Ontario.

The storekeeper of the past was apt to be the only one in the village to own a safe, and as an added service he stored valuables, deeds, wills and other legal documents for his customers. His store was a place where people would gather to hear the latest news, the men chewing tobacco while the storekeeper figured out the value of the produce they brought for barter. On a cold and blustery winter's evening they would be found sitting on a barrel or lingering around a glowing box stove in the store exchanging some gossip with friends and neighbours or contemplating the future and wondering where the world was going.

The Herb Garden

As you pass the Laskay Emporium on the way to the Harness Shop, you encounter one of the many pioneer gardens found at Black Creek Village. You will recognize by the delightful fragances that this one is an old-fashioned herb garden. Over forty varieties of herbs are grown here, the kind of herbs that were commonly used in early Canada for cooking or to concoct remedies for a wide range of ailments and everyday complaints.

Meadowsweet

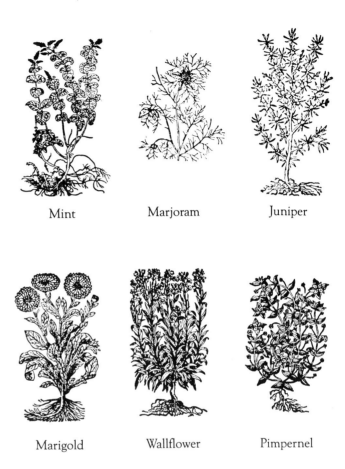

Mint   Marjoram   Juniper

Marigold   Wallflower   Pimpernel

Everyone knew that chewing the leaves of yarrow relieved toothache and that sage brewed as a tea relieved the symptoms of a cold and eased a sore throat. A persistent cough could be helped by smoking rosemary; as a tea, rosemary was considered a cure for headaches; in cooking it was used to flavour meat or stews. Curly mint improved digestion, summer savory could bring a fever down. Comfrey was known to speed the healing of wounds and was applied to broken bones.

The perennial known as "old man" was effective as an antidote for deadly poisons and was also used to restore hair. Winter savory was popular not only as a remedy for colic, but also as a culinary herb as were tarragon, chives and borage.

Tansy soaked in buttermilk was good for a girl's fair complexion. Lavender was thought to cure dropsy; it seemed to help in the case of a fainting spell. The seeds of the annual dill could be chewed in church to relieve boredom when the sermon, as usual, was a long one; and if the minister was not able to drive out devils, the perennial rue was believed to do it. The rue also improved one's sight and was thought to sharpen one's wit.

The Half Way House

The Half Way House at Black Creek Village is a busy place. Food is being prepared in large quantities to serve meals to the inn's patrons. The commodious kitchen is equipped with a large fireplace and the many utensils that befit a well-run 19th century inn. From the inn's bake oven outside in a separate small building wafts the pungent aroma of freshly-baked whole wheat bread.

The inn was the social centre of any village. Farmers, shopkeepers and craftsmen would congregate at the inn's barroom in the evening to have a drink and swap stories. Sometimes an inn like the Half Way House served as a polling station at election time, or as a meeting place for the Sons of Temperance or a congregation while their church was being rebuilt after a fire.

The Half Way House.

Located on the well-travelled Kingston Road, halfway between the settlement of Dunbarton and the St. Lawrence market at Toronto, the Half Way House was a well-known stage coach stop back in the 1850s. Farmers would stop there for food and drink on their way to and from the market.

The inn had a reputation for serving excellent meals. The friendly innkeeper himself most likely was also the bartender in the barroom where his patrons had a couple of beer or a glass or two of whiskey while waiting for their grain to be ground at a nearby mill or their horses shod by the blacksmith.

The Royal Mail

Baking in the kitchen of the Half Way House.

The Grand Trunk Railway, although under construction, was not opened for traffic on the Toronto, Kingston, Montreal route until the fall of 1856, and William Weller's Royal Mail coaches travelling on the King's Highway still had the lucrative mail contract on the Kingston-Toronto run. The driver was sure to stop at an inn like the Half Way House to wash down the dust of the road with a drink and if need be make a quick change of horses.

Travellers wishing overnight accommodation at the inn found comfortable bedrooms waiting at a reasonable rate. Rooms were rented out on a first come, first served basis and when the weather was bad and all rooms were taken, mattresses were put on the floor of the upstairs ballroom. Female travellers would spend the evening after dinner in the inn's "ladies parlour," while the men sat in the barroom discussing rising prices and how to vote in the next election.

A ballroom was a standard feature of most 19th century inns. Although it was seldom used as such, it served as a place for community functions, political meetings and lectures or as a stage for a travelling show.

Sometimes a travelling salesman would rent a room at the inn to display his wares. Or a photographer, having advertised his arrival in the local paper, would use the room as his studio to take pictures of some newlyweds or do a family portrait.

Dickson's Hill School.

Dickson's Hill School

The one-room schoolhouse, once common throughout rural Ontario, has long since disappeared. Education over the years has changed dramatically since the early 1800s when the three "R's," reading, writing and 'rithmetic, were considered sufficient to get by in the world.

Education was not compulsory in those days. In the summer and at harvest time children were needed to help on the farm. Only about one third of Upper Canada's population could read and write. Teachers had no formal training. As their pay amounted to a pittance, they had to rely on the generosity of the families who took turns in boarding them. Many elementary schools were poorly equipped—benches without backs, a wood stove, a water pail and dipper, a wooden board painted black on the wall for writing, a few tattered textbooks, slates and slate pencils for the pupils and a few birch rods for the teacher to keep the discipline.

Government funding was meagre at best, and local authorities had to depend on voluntary contributions by parents to build and maintain a schoolhouse in their community. Granted, for the "sons of gentlemen" there were district grammar schools with boarding facilities, qualified teachers usually chosen from the Anglican clergy, and a curriculum which might include Latin, Greek, algebra and trigonometry. The daughters of affluent settlers were permitted to attend.

Not until the Reverend Egerton Ryerson became head of the Department of Public Instructions, a capacity in which he served from 1846 to 1876, did Ontario's present system of free public education begin to emerge. Ryerson, a Methodist minister and in his early years a circuit rider and missionary to the Native Peoples, was determined to see "every child in my native land in the school-going way."

From "The Pioneers of Old Ontario"

A one-room school in the early days

The 1860 schoolhouse, which was moved to Black Creek from Dickson's Hill in Markham Township, was designed according to Ryerson's recommendations. There are windows on both sides of the classroom to admit plenty of daylight and provide cross-ventilation, but they are located high enough so that the students cannot see out and be distracted from their work. The building has two entrances and separate cloakrooms for boys and girls. The classroom has "central heating" which means the wood stove is located not in the centre as in earlier schoolhouses, but in the back with the stovepipe running all the way to the front to distribute the heat more evenly.

All grades were taught simultaneously in this one-room rural school. Books were still scarce and attendance remained sporadic, especially in the summer. The teacher relied on a large blackboard while the children were drilled in memory work. A fair amount of prose and poetry had to be committed to memory and recited for the teacher. Repetition in unison of facts, dates and figures was considered the best way to retain the lessons. Spelling matches were held frequently and were eagerly anticipated by good students who wanted to show off their skill, but the annual examination which took place under the watchful eye of school trustees was looked forward to with much trepidation not only by students but by their teacher as well.

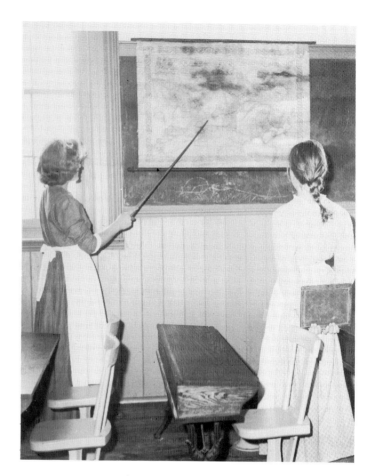

A geography lesson.

Fisherville Church, 1856.

Religious Life

Among the settlers of Upper Canada were people of all faiths and denominations, Anglicans, Presbyterians, Methodists, Baptists, Quakers, Mennonites and Roman Catholics. The Anglicans were by far in the minority, but the Church of England, while not in law acknowledged as the official church, enjoyed nearly all the benefits derived from Clergy Reserves, land set aside "for the support and maintenance of a Protestant clergy." Proceeds from such lands were to be used by the provincial government under the 1791 Constitutional Act for the erection and maintenance of rectories and parsonages "according to the establishment of the Church of England," a provision which by officials was interpreted to exclude all other Protestant denominations.

This caused much discord and grievance, and while the Presbyterians were one group which eventually succeeded in obtaining the right to share in the support derived from the Clergy Reserves, the issue remained a bone of contention in Canadian politics for years to come.

The settlers meanwhile clung to their faith which had sustained them in the first harsh years of isolation in a wilderness land. They met in each others homes for worship, welcoming the itinerant preacher whose circuit often ranged over a couple of hundred miles or more.

The strongest competition for settlers' souls came from the Methodist circuit rider. He was a tough, determined traveller, out in all weather and riding long miles to attend a camp meeting or speak to a few people gathered for his message.

One popular method of reaching large numbers of rural folk was the camp meeting. This was an elaborate gathering, lasting from several days to a fortnight. Benches of slabwood served to seat the congregation, and fences to keep out intruders. Visiting preachers rallied forth from a central platform.

As soon as resources could be found, each denomination was anxious to build its own church in their community. A member of the congregation usually donated the land, and labour to erect the structure was supplied by volunteers. As the congregation prospered and grew, the original plain building was replaced by a more imposing and commodious house of worship and if possible a home was provided for a resident minister and his family. A driveshed near the church was a must to accommodate the horses and buggies of worshippers during church services.

The Edgeley Mennonite Meeting House at Black Creek Village is one of the early places of worship. Built in 1824, it is thought to be the oldest log meeting house still in existence in Ontario. Its exterior is well weathered, and the house contains all its original furnishings.

The Presbyterians of Fisherville built the church which presently serves the inhabitants of Black Creek Pioneer Village. It stood on land owned by Jacob Fisher at the corner of what is now Steeles Avenue and Dufferin Street.

A fine example of Greek Revival architecture, the interior of the Fisherville Church is simply furnished with box pews and a high pulpit. The church is lighted by candles just as it was in 1856 when the building was constructed.

Worshippers used to bring footwarmers in winter to keep comfortable during the long services. Sunday was set aside according to the Bible as a day of rest, and people spent many hours of the day at their church. Here they found relief from their daily grind; their spirit was lifted by the sermon in the morning and again at night. The ladies showed off their new bonnets when neighbours and friends met in front of the church after the service.

Across from the church at Black Creek is the manse. The minister who occupied the house was not a wealthy man, and he and his family relied on the generosity of his congregation for support.

From "The Pioneers of Old Ontario"
A Pioneer Church Service

The Town Hall

The Town Hall

Along with its churches and the schoolhouse, one of the community's most important public buildings is the town hall.

The town hall on Maple Avenue at Black Creek dates from 1858 when it was built for Wilmot Township at Baden, Ontario. Baden by then was a busy town with a railway station, shops and manufacturing establishments.

Before 1849 a governing body of magistrates selected necessary officials such as town warden, clerk and overseer of highways. These in turn determined local needs and expenditures including road works, the building of bridges, police costs and the issuing of tavern licences. This council levied tax rates, heard breach of contract suits, and arranged for local assizes.

After 1849 when the new Municipal Act took effect in Ontario, a new type of municipal government replaced this arrangement. Now an elected township council consisting of a reeve and three councillors took charge of these issues and concerns in local government.

From 1858 on the Wilmot township council was meeting once a month at their new town hall to transact their business. Circuit Judge William Miller presided here over the court called at regular intervals five times a year. The division court settled small claims for debts and damages, contract disputes or a quarrel among neighbours over property rights. Sometimes it would be necessary to call a jury, and five jurors—all male—were selected from a panel of fifteen who had been summoned as prospective candidates. To refuse jury duty carried a fine.

To be chosen as the seat of township government speaks of the growing importance and the progress the village has made. Now the community takes the responsibility for determining many municipal affairs. It represents a coming of age, a movement away from the isolationism of early settlement days.

Black Creek Pioneer Village at the time of Confederation stands on a solid foundation and as an enduring legacy of our pioneer forefathers to this and future generations.

A Woman's Work is Never Done.

A team of horses is patiently waiting outside Daniel Stong's grain barn. The mows are filled with grain, in the centre of the building is the threshing floor, and at the far end the sheep barn.

The Stongs' first home, erected on this site in 1816 near the corner of what later became Jane Street and Steeles Avenue. In the foreground is the piggery with an exercise run for the hogs, built in 1825. Salt pork was the staple of the pioneers' diet and the pigs were slaughtered in late fall of the year.

The farmer is ploughing his field with a yoke of oxen which pull a wooden plough. Superior to horses for heavy work, oxen were also used on the pioneer farm for moving large stumps and stones and clearing the land.

Linen cloth was costly to purchase, so flax was raised by the pioneers to provide for clothing and other necessities. Weeding the flax by hand was just one of the many chores on the farm during the growing season. The coarse fibres were used to make rope and sacks for grain, while the fine silky flax fibres were spun and woven into linen cloth.

Ploughing the field with a team of draught horses

The soil has been tilled and now the winter wheat is broadcast on the ground.

The Stong family's second home, erected in 1832 on this site. The Pennsylvania-German style two-storey house is of hand-hewn timber construction covered with clapboard siding. The front door is the only entrance to the house.

The parents' bedroom with the baby's cradle in the St family's second house.

Roblin's Gristmill with its 18.5 foot overshot waterwheel.

Here at Roblin's gristmill a group of farmers discuss the price of flour with the miller.

Haying time usually begins in June, when the mowers would be in the meadows by sunrise. This farmer with the scythe is ready to go to the fields.

The shearing of sheep takes place in late spring. Most families kept a few sheep to provide wool for blankets and warm clothing.

Reading by kerosene lamp in the sitting room of the Doctor's House. Kerosene lamps did not come into use until after the mid-1800s.

The pioneer housewife was never idle. Spinning sheep's wool into yarn to be woven into cloth was a job done by the women and girls.

Many cords of wood were chopped every year to supply fuel for warmth and comfort, for light to work by and to provide heat for cooking and baking.

The Burwick House at Black Creek Pioneer Village which dates back to the 1840s is one of the most attractive homes in the community. Houses such as this would have been built by the well-to-do, perhaps a retired army officer or a gentleman farmer. The eight rooms of the house are exquisitely furnished with fine pieces, some made in Upper Canada, others brought over from England. The open fireplace in the kitchen is used for cooking, while the baking is done in the brick oven in the adjoining scullery. Stables and a woodshed are located in the back. The well-kept grounds are fenced in, enhancing the gracious appearance of this country residence.

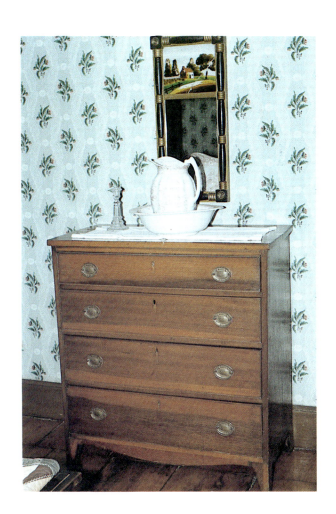

The main bedroom in the Burwick House. The canopy bed is indicative of the wealthy owner's lifestyle.

A chest of drawers at the Burwick House.

Stoking the fire in the kitchen of the Burwick House to cook dinner for the family.

A wholesome breakfast or lunch was home baked whole wheat bread spread with freshly churned butter.

The Printing Office has been established in the north wing of what was once a Temperance Hall in Kettleby, King Township. It is a typical small mid-19th century print shop where broadsides, notices of sales or auctions and the weekly newspaper were produced on the old Washington flat bed press or the more up-to-date cylindrical Hoe press. The newspaper usually consisted of four pages and included some local reports and advertisements and the news from the outside world gleaned from American papers, usually several weeks old before it reached Upper Canada.

The Washington flat bed press on which the picture was printed was first introduced in the 1820s and was still being used by the middle of the 19th century. it was on such a press that William Lyon Mackenzie printed his *Colonial Advocate* on the pages of which the fiery Reformer fought the powerful Family Compact rule of his day.

The new edition of the weekly paper has just come out, and villagers eagerly read the latest news.

Striking while the iron is hot, the blacksmith hammers a horseshoe on his anvil.

Outside his shop the village blacksmith is checking the shoes of the farmer's horses. If needed, he will make new shoes for the team.

Travellers arriving at the Half Way House. In the wintertime, when rivers and lakes were frozen over and the roads packed with snow, travelling by horse-drawn sleigh or cutter was at its best. The passengers would wrap themselves in warm furs and woollen blankets.

Villagers mingle with guests in the barroom of the Half Way House to discuss politics and exchange the village news.

The innkeeper greets his guests at the entrance of the Half Way House. The travellers' horses will have to be stabled and looked after. The blacksmith shop and the harness maker are located nearby should the inn's patrons require their services to replace a horseshoe or a broken harness.

Baking apple pies, sweetened with maple syrup, in the kitchen of the Half Way House. Even back in the old days when the Half Way House was an inn on the well-travelled Kingston Road, the place had a reputation for serving good food to its patrons.

The brick oven in the kitchen of the Half Way House is heating up while the bread dough is rising and the cookies are being shaped. When the bricks are hot, the coals are raked out and the bread is baked first. One **method that the housewife** used to test the temperature was to hold her hand over the hot bricks. If she could only hold her hand in the heat long enough to count to twenty, the heat was just right for baking.

The freshly baked crusty loaves of bread were baked in the outdoor bake oven of the Half Way House. The oven holds 25 loaves at a time. The inn was once located on the Kingston Road, halfway between Dunbarton and the market at Toronto.

Charles Irvine's Weavers Shop shares the premises with the village's printing office. Although some pioneer housewives possessed a loom and did their own weaving, many others only carded, spun and dyed their wool or flax and for the weaving relied on the itinerant weaver visiting their village from time to time. Eventually, however, professional weavers set up their permanent shops in many communities of Upper Canada producing for their customers yard goods and colourful rag rugs on their looms. Some of these weavers employed spinning girls to prepare the yarns for weaving, others took on apprentices to learn the highly skilled craft.

The Mackenzie House, the earliest section of which was built of log in 1837, was enlarged in the 1850's and covered with board and batten. It is the home of the local clockmaker and his wife, the village seamstress. The clockmaker builds and repairs clocks and watches in a little shop set up adjacent to the parlour. His wife works on her treadle sewing machine in the kitchen. Their parlour with its dark walnut furniture reflects the mid-Victorian taste of the 1860s.

Quilting requires small even stitching and the woman took pride in her work. Every girl wished to have several quilts in her hope chest. Friends and neighbours would often gather at each other's houses in the afternoons for a quilting bee, working away on the quilt and exchanging some gossip until the men came home for supper.

The seamstress at the Mackenzie House is using a Wheeler & Wilson treadle sewing machine patented in the 1850s. Note the fabric is fed sideways.

A quilting bee is in progress at the Stong residence. It was pleasant work and a favourite way of socializing with friends back in pioneer days. In the evening husbands and young men would be invited for tea and games. When the quilt was finished the girls might toss it over one of the boys to see how quickly he could untangle himself from the folds.

Small weaver's shops like the one at Black Creek Pioneer Village would make colourful rag rugs to order. Cotton or linen thread is used for the warp and rags, supplied by the customer, for the woof or weft.

At the Weaver's Shop yard goods are produced and rag rugs are made to order. Here at the pirn winder the yarn is wound on the pirn to be put into the shuttle for weaving. The pirn is a device resembling a spool.

Built in the Greek Revival style by the Presbyterians in 1856 on land belonging to Jacob Fisher at the corner of Dufferin Street and Steeles Avenue, the church became the Fisherville United Church in 1925. Of pine frame construction with a roughcast stucco exterior, the church has no steeple.

The interior of the Fisherville Church is simple, even austere. Lighting is provided by candles, and the room is furnished with box pews and a high pulpit. Box pews would keep the young children secure and prevented drafts in winter. Some worshippers brought footwarmers to be more comfortable during the long winter services. In pioneer days, each denomination, no matter how small the membership in the community, took pride in building its own house of worship. Later, as the congregation increased, the old church might be replaced by a more imposing structure.

The Laskay Emporium, built by a prosperous miller in Laskay, Ontario in 1856, was stocked with a wide variety of goods, clothing, shoes, china, glass, barrels of sugar or molasses, groceries, cigars and snuff, boxes of soap, spirits, medicines and hardware, and all the luxuries a farmer could not produce himself. Bringing his farm produce—butter, eggs, grain or pork—to the store, he would barter for the ready-made, often imported goods and articles. Here at the general store the men would gather after the day's hard work to discuss the weather, the news and politics or pick up the mail at the post office located at the rear of the store.

Barrels made by the cooper were the containers of the day in the 1800s. Everything from molasses, sugar, grain, apples, whiskey and flour was shipped in barrels. Here a delivery arrives at the Laskay Emporium.

The Dominion Carriage Works, once located in the Stratford area, houses a blacksmith and wheelwright shop. At the carriage works new wagons and carriages were built and vehicles of all types were repaired.

The cabinet maker has made a new chair for one of his customers. A skilled craftsman, he would make furniture of all types to order. At times called upon to make coffins, he sometimes became the local undertaker.

The Dickson's Hill School, a one-room schoolhouse dating back to 1861, was built in the Markham area to a design recommended by Egerton Ryerson, Superintendent of Education and founder of Ontario's public school system. The building, heated in winter by a wood stove, has separate entrances and cloak rooms for boys and girls. Note the British flag on the pole in the yard.

Today's students and their teacher come for a week to the old one-room school at Black Creek Pioneer Village to learn about their country's past. They use slates and slate pencils just like the students did a century ago, and when school is out, they visit the shops and houses in the village.

The Doctor's House, originally a farm home built in Chinguacousy Township, was restored to represent a typical country doctor's residence at the time of Confederation. Of frame construction, the house has two separate sections, one used for the doctor's office, the other for his living quarters. Trees are shading the well-kept grounds and the medicinal herb garden which surrounds the house.

The country doctor was often a dentist as well; here he examines a patient's teeth.

The doctor's herb garden which surrounds his house contains more than 180 varieties used for medicinal purposes.

The medicine cupboard at the doctor's office.

The doctor's housekeeper covers the fireplace with an ornamental screen.

Picking herbs in the herb garden near the Laskay Emporium. Thyme, sage, savory, fennel, caraway were some of the many varieties collected in the fall to be dried for use in winter.

The Pennsylvania-German type vegetable garden, surrounded by a wooden fence to keep out the chickens, pigs and other animals, is located behind Daniel Stong's second house. The square beds are edged by boards and separated by one or two paths in the centre and a path running along the sides.

To avoid heating the house in summer, skeins of wool are often dyed outside in an iron kettle over an open fire. Onion skins or golden rod could be used for yellow, sumach blossoms for brown, and the bark of the beech tree for drab.

Making candles for the long winter months, either by dipping or moulding, was an important job to be carried out in the fall of the year when tallow (animal fat) was available after the fall butchering. Braided cotton wicking was attached to a stick and dipped into the melted tallow. The process of dipping was repeated after the tallow hardened on the wick until the desired thickness of the candle was obtained.

A view of the Stong farm complex in its peaceful setting on a clear winter's day. In the background is the five-storey stone gristmill of the village.

The tinsmith at work in his shop repairing and making all kinds of household utensils. Not easily broken, tin and pewter ware was economical to use.

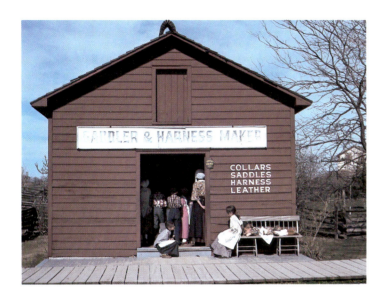

At the Harness Shop and Saddlery all kinds of leather articles including harnesses and saddle gear, trunks and bags, and leather aprons were hand crafted or repaired.

Harnessmaking was an essential trade at a time when everyone depended on the horse and buggy for transportation. A thorough knowledge of the properties of various leathers was required, and occasionally the harnessmaker would also be a tanner. Here at the harnessmaker's shop a saddle is being repaired. In the background hang sleigh bells used for travelling through the otherwise silent winter landscape.

Inside the gunsmith shop an apprentice is checking the stock for a new gun. Several hundred more hours of work by the gunsmith will be needed before the gun is completed. A gunsmith had to be a multi-talented person. His apprenticeship with a master would have lasted seven or eight years, and he would have to learn to work with wood as well as metal. Consequently, he would have to use cabinetmaking, blacksmithing and even silversmithing skills to complete a gun. In addition he needed to acquire the skills of a locksmith which would enable him to make and repair the gun's firing mechanism.

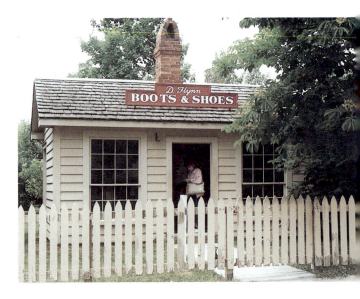

This small boot and shoe shop was built by Daniel Flynn in the late 1850s, at Newtonbrook, Ontario. Originally Flynn, like most of the early boot and shoe makers in Upper Canada, would have been itinerant travelling from farm to farm, boarding with a family as long as it took to repair and make new shoes for each family member.

The shoe and boot maker at work in his little shop repairing and occasionally making new shoes to order for his customers. On the wall are patterns, lasts and on his cobbler's bench some tools of his trade. He would have learned his craft working several years for a master shoemaker first as apprentice and then as journeyman.

A batchelor broom maker resides in this one-room log house dating back to the 1840s. It now houses his broom making machine along with the basic furnishings of his living quarters. In the attic of the dwelling he stores the broom corn needed for his trade.

Inside the broom maker's workshop and living quarters. Here on the broom making machine the young man is being shown how to make a broom, a relatively simple process which he can learn in a short period of time. By mid-19th century broom corn which previously had to be imported from south of the border was being grown extensively in Ontario and broom making became a thriving cottage industry.

The shop of the gunsmith is located on Maple Avenue at Black Creek Pioneer Village. The building once stood in the village of Bolton, Ontario. Early settlers, depending on wild game for their meat, needed guns, and the gunsmith had to repair imported guns as well as make new firearms.

The Town Hall along with the church and the village schoolhouse is one of the community's important public buildings. It is the seat of township government and here council meetings and other assemblies would be held. The circuit judge would preside over court here at regular intervals to deal with small claims cases or to settle disputes between the inhabitants over breach of contracts not exceeding the amount of $100. The hall was built for Wilmot Township in 1858 at Baden, Ontario.

The table in the dining room of the doctor's house is set for tea with fine imported china.

The table is set in the elegant dining room of the Burwick House with the fine china imported from England. It is Christmas time, and the mantle of the fireplace is decorated with boughs of evergreen and berries.

The Christmas tree is set up in the kitchen of the Stong family's second house where most of the family's daily activities are centred. The Christmas cookies are baking in the open fireplace, and the room is cozy and warm, filled with the inviting fragrance of spices.

The children help decorate the Christmas tree, already laden with strings of popcorn, gingerbread cookies and homemade fleece ornaments. Cranberries which used to grow in the marshlands of Upper Canada made colourful chains that are draped over the branches. Some practical presents such as knitted mittens and hats are on the tree as gifts for the children.

Apples for cider were crushed in this hand-operated cider mill. Some of the cider was used to make apple butter. Some was stored in wooden barrels and later served as a drink. If the temperature of the stored cider rose above 59 degrees Fahrenheit, it turned to vinegar which was used for pickling and cooking.

Bibliography

Armstrong, F. H. et al. (eds.), *Aspects of Nineenth-Century Ontario*. Toronto: University of Toronto Press, 1974.

Byers, Mary et al., *Rural Roots*. Toronto: University of Toronto Press, 1977.

"Canuck, A." *Early Life in Upper Canada*. Toronto: William Briggs, 1905.

Craig, Gerald (ed.), *Early Travellers in the Canadas*. Toronto: Macmillan, 1968.

Duncan, Dorothy, "Black Creek Pioneer Village," (n.d.,n.p.).

Guillet, Edwin C., *Pioneer Arts and Crafts*. Toronto: University of Toronto Press, 1973.

Guillet, Edwin C., *Pioneer Days in Upper Canada*. Toronto: University of Toronto Press, 1975.

Guillet, Edwin C., *The Pioneer Farmer and Backwoodsman*. Vols. I, II. Toronto: University of Toronto Press, 1970.

Glazebrook, G. P. deT., *Life in Ontario: A Social History*. Toronto: University of Toronto Press, 1968.

Haight, Canniff, *Country Life in Canada, Fifty Years Ago*. (facsmile edition) Belleville: Mika Publishing Company, 1977.

Hart, Patrica W., *Pioneering in North York*. Toronto: General Publishing Co. Ltd., 1968.

Herrington, Walter S., *History of the County of Lennox and Addington*. (facsmile edition) Belleville: Mika Publishing Company, 1972.

Langdon, Eustella, *Pioneer Gardens at Black Creek Pioneer Village*. Toronto: Holt, Rinehart and Winston, 1972.

Langton, H.H., (ed.), *A Gentlewoman in Upper Canada: The Journals of Anne Langton*. Toronto: Clarke, Irwin & Company, 1950.

MacDermont, H., *One Hundred Years of Medicine in Canada, 1867–1967*. Toronto: McCelland & Stewart, 1967.

McKendry, Ruth, *Quilts and Other Bed Coverings in the Canadian Tradition*. Toronto: Van Nostrand Reinhold Ltd., 1979.

Mika, Nick and Helma, *Historic Mills of Ontario*. Belleville: Mika Publishing Company, 1987.

Minhinnick, Jeanne, *At Home in Upper Canada*. Toronto: Clarke, Irwin & Company, 1983.

Priamo, Carol, *Mills of Canada*. Toronto: McGraw-Hill Ryerson, 1976.

Reaman, G. Elmore, *The Trail of the Black Walnut*. Toronto: McClelland & Stewart. 1957.

Russell, Loris, *Everyday Life in Colonial Canada*. Toronto: Copp Clark Publishing Company, 1973.

Smith, W.L., *The Pioneers of Old Ontario*. Toronto: George N. Morang, 1923.

Traill, Catharine Parr, *The Backwoods of Canada*. (reprinted) Toronto: McClelland & Stewart, 1966.

Traill, Catharine Parr, *The Canadian Settler's Guide*. (reprinted) Toronto: McClelland & Steward.

Webster, Donald Blake (ed.), *The Book of Canadian Antiques*. Toronto: McGraw-Hill Ryerson, 1974.

Williams, David M., *Early Days in Upper Canada*. Toronto: Gage Educational Publishing Ltd. 1972.

Index

Anglicans, 53
apple orchard, 21, 27, 38
Ameliasburg (ON), 29
American Revolution, 33

Baden (ON), 55, 100
bake kettle, 26
bake oven, 26, 48
baking bread, 26
Baldwin, Joseph, 46
ballroom, (see inn)
Baptists, 53
barn, 22, 23
barn raising bee, 22, 23
bartering, (barter) 28, 45, 46
Black Creek, 30, 38
Black Creek Village Printing Office, 36, 37
Black Rock, 16
blacksmith (smithy), 31, 33, 48, 70, 71
blacksmith shop, 16, 71, 74, 86
board and batten construction, 31, 77
Bolton (ON), 33, 100
boot and shoe shop, 38
Brampton (ON), 43
Britain, 20
British Crown, 16
broom corn, 34, 99
broom maker, 15, 34, 99
Burwick (see Woodbridge),
Burwick House (Home), 13, 39-42, 66-68, 101
butter churning, 25

cabinetmaker, 32, 33, 87
Cabinetmaker's shop, 33
Canada West, 34
candle making, 25, 94
carpenter, 23
chaff, 24
cheese, 25
    "Schmier Kase", 25
cheese making, 25
Chinguacousy Township, 90
church, 28, 48, 53, 83, 100
Church of England, 53
church service, 54
cider mill, 27, 38, 95
cider-making bees, 38
circuit judge, 100
circuit rider (preacher), 51, 53
clockmaker, 44, 45, 77
cobbler, 39, 98
Clergy Reserves, 37, 53
Clydesdales, 31
Cobourg (ON), 15
coffin, 33, 87
Colonial Advocate, 37, 69
Confederation, 16, 44, 55, 90
Constitutional Act (1791), 53
cooper, 34, 85
Cooper, Russell King, 7, 8
cooperage, 34
corduroy roads, 31
corn husking, 22, 24
cottage industry, 34, 99
councillors, 55

Country Life in Canada, 18, 21
cutter, 31, 40, 72

Dalziel barn, 23
dentist, 91
Department of Public Instructions, 51
Dickinson's Hill (settlement), 52
Dickinson's Hill School, 13, 50, 88
distillery (distilleries), 20
divison court, 55
doctor, 42, 43, 91, 92
Doctor's House, 42, 43, 64, 90, 101
Dominion Carriage Works, 13, 32, 33, 86
dowry pieces, 28
dowry boxes, 33
Dufferin Street, 54, 82
dulcimer, 27
Dunbarton (settlement), 48, 76
Dundas Street, 21
"dye garden", 36

1837 Rebellion, 37
Edgeley Mennonite Meeting House, 13, 54
Elia (Pennsylvania German settlement), 38
England, 16, 33, 66, 101

Family Compact, 37, 69
farm(s), 16, 17, 25, 28, 39, 58
farmer(s), 25, 29, 30, 34, 39, 43, 45, 48, 58, 63, 71, 84

105

farmer's wife, 25, 27
fireplace, 18, 19, 26, 34, 39, 40, 48, 66, 92
Fisher, Catherine Hommen, 17
Fisher, Elizabeth (see Elizabeth Stong),
Fisher, Jacob, 54, 82
Fisher, John, 17
Fisherville, (ON), 54
Fisherville Church, 13, 53, 54, 82, 83
flax, 22, 35, 59, 77
flail, 23
flour, 30, 45, 63, 85
"flying shuttle" loom, 36
Flynn, Daniel, 13, 38, 39, 98
Fort Erie (ON), 16
furniture, 39, 40,
    Chippendale, 39
    Regency, 39
    Sheraton, 39

Galloway oxen, 15, 31
general store, 20, 28, 34, 45, 46, 84
gentleman farmer, 66
Gordon press, 36
grain, 23, 24, 29, 30, 48, 84, 85
    barley, 20
    oats, 20
    rye, 20
    wheat, 20, 23, 24, 30
grain barn, 16, 20, 22–24, 57
    granary, 23, 24
    grain mow, 23, 57
    hay mow, 23
    threshing flour, 23, 24, 57
granary (see grain barn), 24
gridiron, 19

Grand Trunk Railway, 50
gristmill, 15, 28, 29, 48, 103
gunsmith, 33, 34, 45, 97, 100

Haight, Canniff, 18, 21, 23, 28
Half Way House, 13, 15, 48-50, 72–76
Harness Shop and Saddlery, 13, 32, 47, 97
harness maker, 32, 74, 97
herb garden, 28, 44, 47, 90-92
herbs, 19, 28, 47, 92
Hoe press, 69
hope chest, 28, 78
horses, 15, 19, 20, 24, 31, 48, 50, 57, 58, 71, 74
    carriage, 40
    draught, 60
Huntington County (Pennsylvania), 16
husking bee, 24

immigrants, 33, 35
Indian corn, 34
inn, 48, 50, 74
    ballroom, 50
innkeeper, 48, 74
Irvine, Charles, 13, 36, 77

James, William, 43
Jane Street, 15, 57
jurors, 55
jury, 55
jury duty, 55
Kerosene lamp, 64
Kettleby (ON), 35, 69
King George III, 16

King Township, 69
Kingston (ON), 44, 50
Kingston Road, 48, 74, 76
kissing game, 24
kitchen, 18, 19, 26, 27, 41, 43, 48, 49, 66, 68, 75
    scullery, 41, 66
kitchen garden, 28, 92

Lake Ontario, 17
Laskay (ON), 46, 84
Laskay Emporium and Post Office, 13, 15, 45-47, 84, 85, 92
Leicester sheep, 21
livestock, 23, 24, 28, 34
locksmith, 97
log house, 99
    dovetailed corners, 17
    oiled paper, 18
    shingles, 18
    squared logs, 17
Loyalists (United Empire Loyalists), 16

Mackenzie, Addison Alexander (Major), 44
Mackenzie, William Lyon, 37, 69
Mackenzie House (Black Creek), 13, 44, 77, 78
manse, 54
Maple Avenue (Black Creek), 55, 100
Markham (ON), 88
Markam Township, 17, 52
Masons of Ontario, 35
    Heritage Lodge, 35
Masonic Lodge, 13, 35
Masonic Order, 35

Mennonites, 53
Methodists, 53
Methodist circuit rider,
Metropolitan Toronto and Region Conservation Authority (now The Toronto and Regional Conservation Authority), 16
Mill Road (Black Creek Pioneer Village), 15
miller, 30, 31, 63, 84
Miller, William (Circuit Judge), 55
mill pond, 30
millstones, 30
millwright, 30
minister, 54
missionary, 51
Moodie, Susanna, 18
Montreal, 29, 44, 50
Municipal Act (1849), 55

Natives (Native People), 42, 51
New England, 20, 34
Newtonbrook (ON), 39, 98
Nobleton (ON), 31

one-room schoolhouse, 15, 28, 50-52, 88, 89, 100
Ontario, 15, 16, 35, 36, 37, 50, 51, 55, 88, 99
ox (oxen), 16, 19, 20, 24, 58
Paris (ON), 30, 34
parlour(s), 27, 28, 44, 45, 77
patent medicines, 44
Pennsylvania, 16
Pennsylvania German settlers, 16, 17, 25, 27, 38, 44

pewter wave, 96
photographer, 50
Pickering Township, 17
piggery, 16, 19, 57
"Pioneers of Old Ontario, The," 22, 24, 25, 31, 51, 54
pirn, 81
pirn winder, 81
pit-saw, 31
polling station, 48
post office, 46, 84
postmaster, 46
potash, 20
preacher, 53
Presbyterians, 53, 54, 82
Prince Edward County, 29
print shop, 69
printer(s), 37, 38, 46
Printing Office, 69, 77

Quakers, 53
Queen Street (Black Creek), 7, 15
quern, 29
quilts, 28, 39, 78, 79
quilting bees, 22, 28, 78, 79

railway(s), 32, 46
reeve, 55
refugees, 33
Revolutionary War, 16
Richmond Hill Manse, 13
Roblin, Owen, 29, 30
Roblin's Gristmill (Mill), 13, 15, 29, 30, 63
Roman Catholics, 53
Royal Mail, 49

Royal Mail coaches, 50
Ryerson, Egerton (Reverend), 51, 52, 88

1791 Constitutional Act, 53
sampler, 27
sauerkraut, 27
sawmill, 18, 31, 32, 46
sawyer, 32
Scarborough Township, 17
seamstress, 44, 77, 78
"schmier kase" (see cheese)
school trustees, 52
schoolhouse (see one-room schoolhouse)
schoolmaster, 15
scullery (see kitchen)
sheaves (grain), 22
sheep, 21
sheep shearing, 21, 64
shoemaker, 39, 98
Simcoe, John Graves (Lt. Gov.), 16
silversmith, 34
smokehouse(s), 16, 19, 24
Snider, Henry, 13, 38
soap making, 25, 26
Sons of Temperance, 35, 48
spelling bee, 15
spider, 19
spinner, 21, 22
spinning wool, 21, 22, 65
spinning-wheel, 21, 22, 33
spit, 19
storekeeper, 45, 46
St. Lawrence Market (Toronto), 48
steampower, 29

Steeles Avenue, 15, 54, 57, 82
Stratford (ON), 33, 86
Stong, Elizabeth (Fisher), 16-18, 27, 28
Stong, Daniel, 13-19, 21-23, 26, 27, 57, 62, 92
Stong farm complex, 103
Stong Home (house), 14, 18, 19, 26, 62, 79, 102

tanner, 32, 97
Taylor Cooperage, 13, 34
teachers, 51, 52, 89
Temperance Hall, 35, 36, 69
thresher, 24
threshing flour (see grain barn)
threshing machine, 23
tin, 34
tin lanterns, 24
tinsmith, 34, 96
Tinsmith Shop, 34, 35
toasting fork, 19

toleware, 34
Toronto (ON), 15, 16, 44, 46, 50, 76
Toronto Nursery, 21
Town Hall, 13, 55, 100
township council, 55
travelling salesman, 50

United Empire Loyalist, 29
United States, 16, 29, 33
Upper Canada, 16-22, 25, 26, 29, 30, 33-35, 37, 44, 51, 53, 66, 69, 77, 98, 102
undertaker, 33, 87
upholsterer, 33

Vaughan Township, 16, 17

War of 1812, 17
Washington flat bed press, 36, 69
water turbine, 30
Waterloo County, 17
waterpower, 29

waterwheel, 29, 30
weaver, 35, 36, 77, 80
Weaver's Shop, 35, 36, 77, 81
Weller, William, 50
West York, 17
Wheeler & Wilson treadle sewing machine, 78
wheelwright, 33
wheelwright shop, 33, 86
Whitechurch Township, 17
Wilmot Township, 55, 100
winnowing, 24
winter wheat, 61
Woodbridge (Burwick) (ON), 39, 44
wool, 21
woollen mill, 46

yoke, 20, 58
Yonge Sreet, 16
York County, 16, 17
York Township, 17